On the Invocation
of the Name of Jesus

On the Invocation of the Name of Jesus

by Lev Gillet,
a Monk of the Eastern Church

Templegate Publishers
Springfield, Illinois
1985

CONTENTS

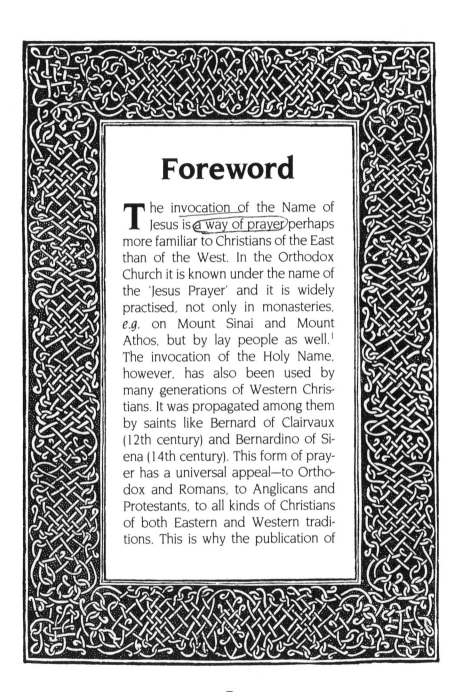

Foreword

T he invocation of the Name of
Jesus is a way of prayer perhaps
more familiar to Christians of the East
than of the West. In the Orthodox
Church it is known under the name of
the 'Jesus Prayer' and it is widely
practised, not only in monasteries,
e.g. on Mount Sinai and Mount
Athos, but by lay people as well.[1]
The invocation of the Holy Name,
however, has also been used by
many generations of Western Christians. It was propagated among them
by saints like Bernard of Clairvaux
(12th century) and Bernardino of Si-
ena (14th century). This form of prayer has a universal appeal—to Orthodox and Romans, to Anglicans and
Protestants, to all kinds of Christians
of both Eastern and Western tradi-
tions. This is why the publication of

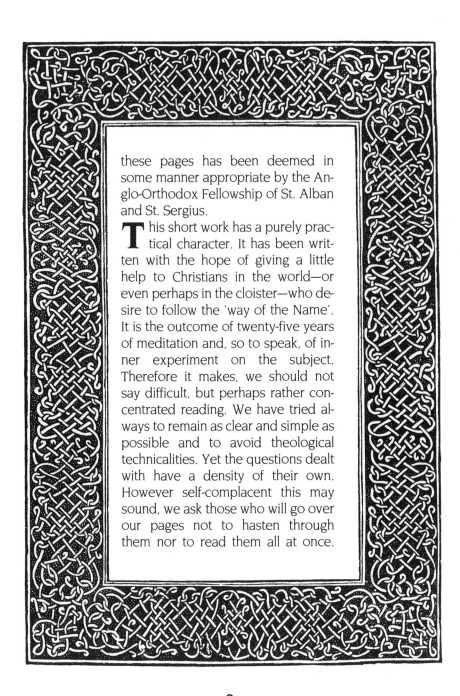

these pages has been deemed in some manner appropriate by the Anglo-Orthodox Fellowship of St. Alban and St. Sergius.

T his short work has a purely practical character. It has been written with the hope of giving a little help to Christians in the world—or even perhaps in the cloister—who desire to follow the 'way of the Name'. It is the outcome of twenty-five years of meditation and, so to speak, of inner experiment on the subject. Therefore it makes, we should not say difficult, but perhaps rather concentrated reading. We have tried always to remain as clear and simple as possible and to avoid theological technicalities. Yet the questions dealt with have a density of their own. However self-complacent this may sound, we ask those who will go over our pages not to hasten through them nor to read them all at once.

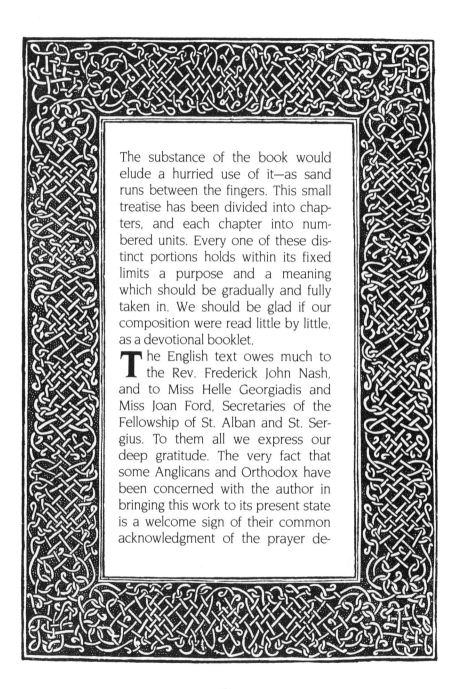

The substance of the book would elude a hurried use of it—as sand runs between the fingers. This small treatise has been divided into chapters, and each chapter into numbered units. Every one of these distinct portions holds within its fixed limits a purpose and a meaning which should be gradually and fully taken in. We should be glad if our composition were read little by little, as a devotional booklet.

The English text owes much to the Rev. Frederick John Nash, and to Miss Helle Georgiadis and Miss Joan Ford, Secretaries of the Fellowship of St. Alban and St. Sergius. To them all we express our deep gratitude. The very fact that some Anglicans and Orthodox have been concerned with the author in bringing this work to its present state is a welcome sign of their common acknowledgment of the prayer de-

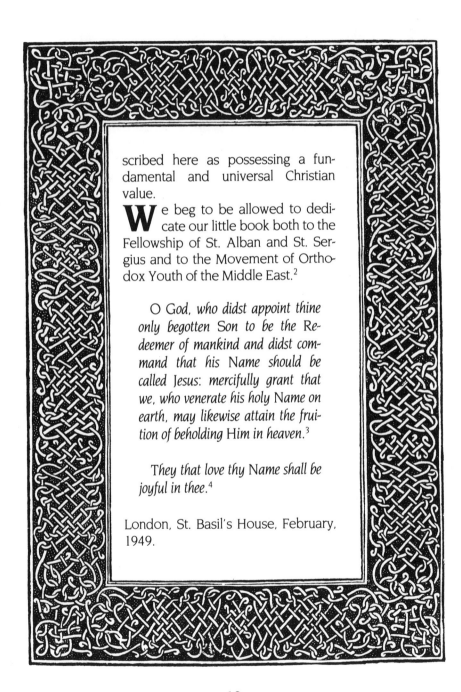

scribed here as possessing a fundamental and universal Christian value.

We beg to be allowed to dedicate our little book both to the Fellowship of St. Alban and St. Sergius and to the Movement of Orthodox Youth of the Middle East.[2]

O God, who didst appoint thine only begotten Son to be the Redeemer of mankind and didst command that his Name should be called Jesus: mercifully grant that we, who venerate his holy Name on earth, may likewise attain the fruition of beholding Him in heaven.[3]

They that love thy Name shall be joyful in thee.[4]

London, St. Basil's House, February, 1949.

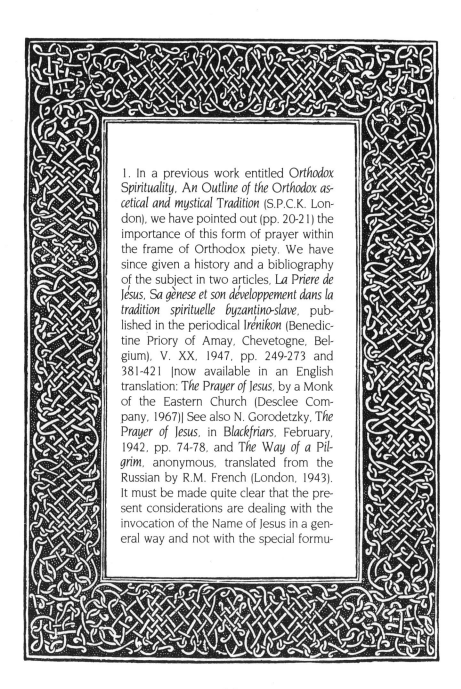

1. In a previous work entitled *Orthodox Spirituality, An Outline of the Orthodox ascetical and mystical Tradition* (S.P.C.K. London), we have pointed out (pp. 20-21) the importance of this form of prayer within the frame of Orthodox piety. We have since given a history and a bibliography of the subject in two articles, *La Priere de Jésus, Sa gènese et son développement dans la tradition spirituelle byzantino-slave*, published in the periodical *Irénikon* (Benedictine Priory of Amay, Chevetogne, Belgium), V. XX, 1947, pp. 249-273 and 381-421 |now available in an English translation: *The Prayer of Jesus*, by a Monk of the Eastern Church (Desclee Company, 1967)| See also N. Gorodetzky, *The Prayer of Jesus*, in *Blackfriars*, February, 1942, pp. 74-78, and *The Way of a Pilgrim*, anonymous, translated from the Russian by R.M. French (London, 1943). It must be made quite clear that the present considerations are dealing with the invocation of the Name of Jesus in a general way and not with the special formu-

las and methods of the Byzantine Jesus
Prayer.
2. The headquarters of which are in Bei-
rut (Lebanon).
3. Roman Missal, collect for the feast of
the Holy Name of Jesus.
4. Psalm 5:12.

I.
The Shape of the Invocation of the Name

And Jacob asked him and said: Tell me, I pray thee, thy name.
And he said: Wherefore is it that thou dost ask after my name?
And he blessed him there.

Genesis 32:29.

1. The invocation of the Name of Jesus can be put into many frames. It is for each person to find the form which is the most appropriate to his or her own prayer. But, whatever formula may be used, the heart and centre of the invocation must be the Holy Name itself, the word *Jesus*. There resides the whole strength of the invocation.

2. The Name of Jesus may either be used alone or be inserted in a more or less developed phrase. In the East the commonest form is: 'Lord Jesus Christ, Son of God, have mercy upon me, a sinner'. One might simply say: 'Jesus Christ', or 'Lord Jesus'. The invocation may even be reduced to one single word, 'Jesus'.

3. This last form—the Name of Jesus only—is the most ancient mould of the invocation of the Name. It is the shortest, the simplest and, as we think, the easiest. Therefore, without deprecating the other formulas, we suggest that the word 'Jesus' alone should be used.

4. Thus, when we speak of the invocation of the Name, we mean the devout and frequent repetition of the Name itself, of the word 'Jesus' without additions. The Holy

14

Name is the prayer.

5. The Name of Jesus may be either pronounced or silently thought. In both cases there is a real invocation of the Name, verbal in the first case, and purely mental in the second. This prayer affords an easy transition from verbal to mental prayer. Even the verbal repetition of the Name, if it is slow and thoughtful, makes us pass to mental prayer and disposes the soul to contemplation.

II.
The Practice of the Invocation of the Name

And I will wait on thy name.

Psalm 52:9.

6. The invocation of the Name may be practised anywhere and at any time. We can pronounce the Name of Jesus in the streets, in the place of our work, in our room, in church, etc. We can repeat the Name while we walk. Besides that 'free' use of the Name, not determined or limited by any rule, it is good to set apart certain times and certain places for a 'regular' invocation of the Name. One who is advanced in that way of prayer may dispense with such arrangements. But they are an almost necessary condition for beginners.

7. If we daily assign a certain time to the invocation of the Name (besides the 'free' invocation which should be as frequent as possible), the invocation ought to be practised—circumstances allowing—in a lonely and quiet place: 'Thou, when thou prayest, enter into thine inner chamber, and, when thou hast shut thy door, pray to thy Father which is in secret'.[1] The bodily posture does not matter much. One may walk, or sit down, or lie, or kneel. The best posture is the one which affords most physical quiet and inner concentration. One may be helped by a physical attitude expressing humbleness and worship.

8. Before beginning to pronounce the Name of Jesus, establish-peace and recollection within yourself and ask for the inspiration and guidance of the Holy Ghost. 'No man can say that Jesus is the Lord, but by the Holy Ghost'.[2] The Name of Jesus cannot really enter a heart that is not being filled by the cleansing breath and the flame of the Spirit. The Spirit himself will breathe and light in us the Name of the Son.

9. Then simply begin. In order to walk one must take a first step; in order to swim one must throw oneself into the water. It is the same with the invocation of the Name. Begin to pronounce it with adoration and love. Cling to it. Repeat it. Do not think that you are invoking the Name; think only of Jesus himself. Say his Name slowly, softly and quietly.

10. A common mistake of beginners is to wish to associate the invocation of the Holy Name with inner intensity or emotion. They try to say it with great force. But the Name of Jesus is not to be shouted, or fashioned with violence, even inwardly. When Elijah was commanded to stand before the Lord, there was a great and strong wind, but the Lord was not in the wind; and after the wind an earthquake, but the Lord was not in the earthquake; and after the earthquake a fire, but the Lord was not in the fire. After the fire came a still small voice, 'And it was so, when Elijah heard it, that he wrapped his face in his mantle, and went out, and stood...'[3] Strenuous exertion and the search for intensity will be of no avail. As you repeat the Holy Name, gather quietly, little by little, your thoughts and feelings and will around it; gather around it your whole being. Let the Name penetrate your soul as a drop of oil spreads out and impregnates a cloth. Let nothing of yourself escape. Surrender your whole self and enclose it within the Name.

11. Even in the act of invocation of the Name, its literal repetition ought not to be continuous. The Name pronounced may be extended and prolonged in seconds or minutes of silent rest and attention. The repetition of the Name may be likened to the beating of wings by which a bird rises into the air. It must never be laboured and forced, or hurried, or in the nature of a flapping. It must be gentle, easy, and—let us give to this word its deepest meaning—graceful. When the bird has reached the desired height it glides in its flight, and only beats its wing from time to time in order to stay in the air. So the soul, having attained to the thought of Jesus and filled herself with the memory of him may discontinue the repetition of the Name and

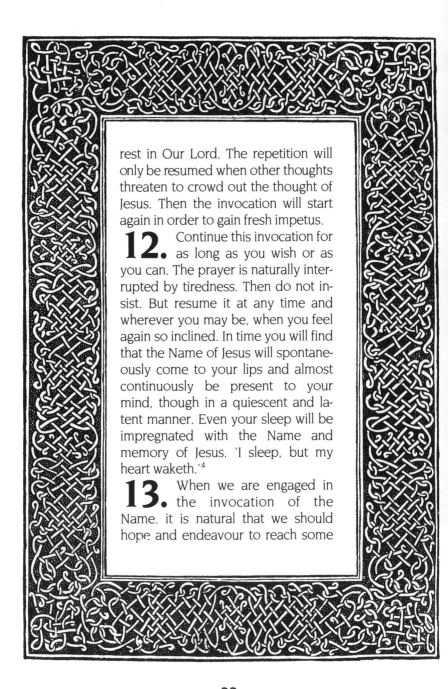

rest in Our Lord. The repetition will only be resumed when other thoughts threaten to crowd out the thought of Jesus. Then the invocation will start again in order to gain fresh impetus.

12. Continue this invocation for as long as you wish or as you can. The prayer is naturally interrupted by tiredness. Then do not insist. But resume it at any time and wherever you may be, when you feel again so inclined. In time you will find that the Name of Jesus will spontaneously come to your lips and almost continuously be present to your mind, though in a quiescent and latent manner. Even your sleep will be impregnated with the Name and memory of Jesus. 'I sleep, but my heart waketh.'[4]

13. When we are engaged in the invocation of the Name. it is natural that we should hope and endeavour to reach some

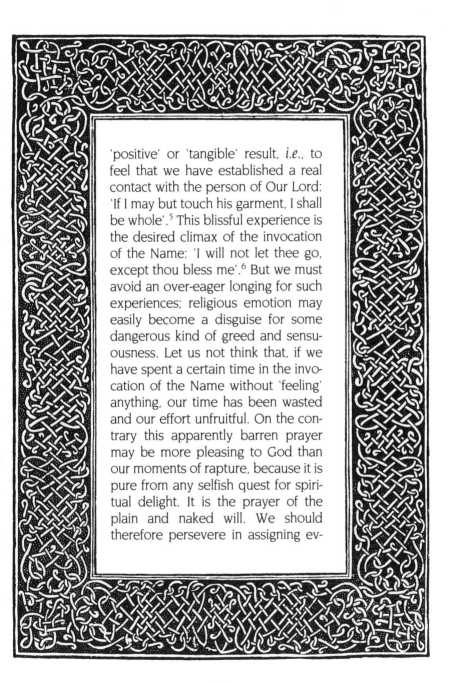

'positive' or 'tangible' result, *i.e.*, to feel that we have established a real contact with the person of Our Lord: 'If I may but touch his garment, I shall be whole'.[5] This blissful experience is the desired climax of the invocation of the Name: 'I will not let thee go, except thou bless me'.[6] But we must avoid an over-eager longing for such experiences; religious emotion may easily become a disguise for some dangerous kind of greed and sensuousness. Let us not think that, if we have spent a certain time in the invocation of the Name without 'feeling' anything, our time has been wasted and our effort unfruitful. On the contrary this apparently barren prayer may be more pleasing to God than our moments of rapture, because it is pure from any selfish quest for spiritual delight. It is the prayer of the plain and naked will. We should therefore persevere in assigning ev-

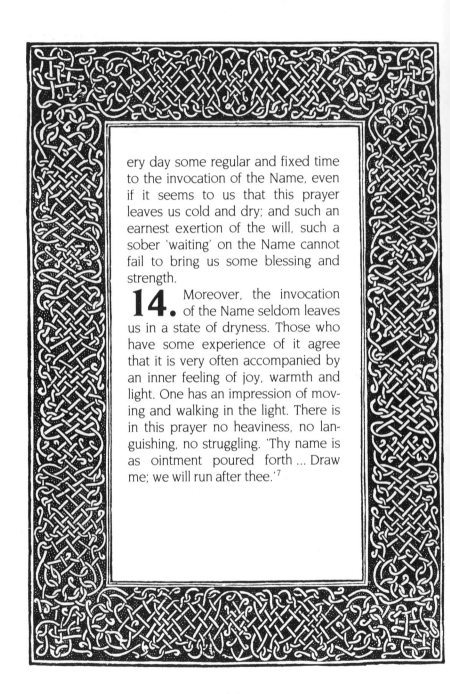

ery day some regular and fixed time to the invocation of the Name, even if it seems to us that this prayer leaves us cold and dry; and such an earnest exertion of the will, such a sober 'waiting' on the Name cannot fail to bring us some blessing and strength.

14. Moreover, the invocation of the Name seldom leaves us in a state of dryness. Those who have some experience of it agree that it is very often accompanied by an inner feeling of joy, warmth and light. One has an impression of moving and walking in the light. There is in this prayer no heaviness, no languishing, no struggling. 'Thy name is as ointment poured forth ... Draw me; we will run after thee.'[7]

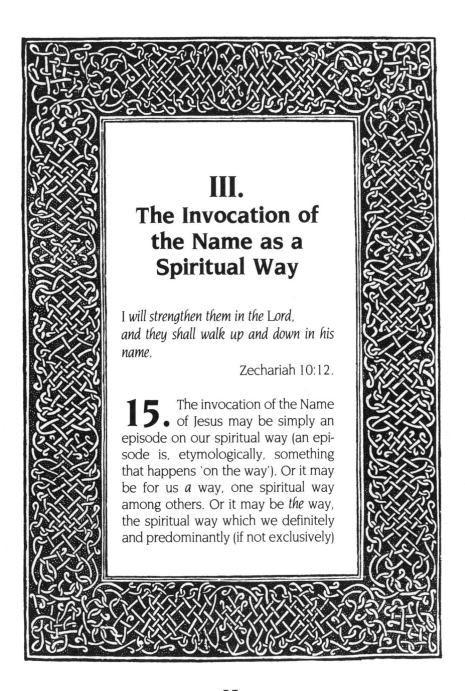

III.
The Invocation of the Name as a Spiritual Way

I will strengthen them in the Lord,
and they shall walk up and down in his
name.

Zechariah 10:12.

15. The invocation of the Name of Jesus may be simply an episode on our spiritual way (an episode is, etymologically, something that happens 'on the way'). Or it may be for us *a* way, one spiritual way among others. Or it may be *the* way, the spiritual way which we definitely and predominantly (if not exclusively)

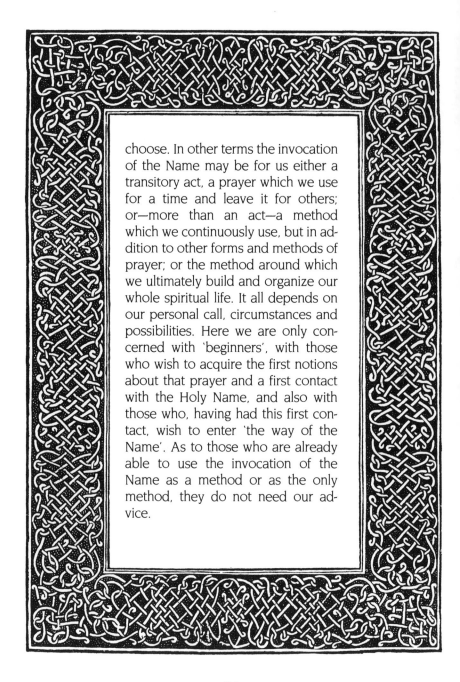

choose. In other terms the invocation of the Name may be for us either a transitory act, a prayer which we use for a time and leave it for others; or—more than an act—a method which we continuously use, but in addition to other forms and methods of prayer; or the method around which we ultimately build and organize our whole spiritual life. It all depends on our personal call, circumstances and possibilities. Here we are only concerned with 'beginners', with those who wish to acquire the first notions about that prayer and a first contact with the Holy Name, and also with those who, having had this first contact, wish to enter 'the way of the Name'. As to those who are already able to use the invocation of the Name as a method or as the only method, they do not need our advice.

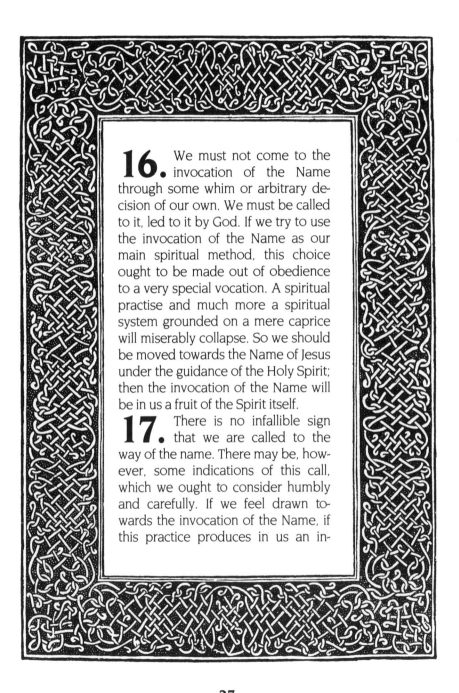

16. We must not come to the invocation of the Name through some whim or arbitrary decision of our own. We must be called to it, led to it by God. If we try to use the invocation of the Name as our main spiritual method, this choice ought to be made out of obedience to a very special vocation. A spiritual practise and much more a spiritual system grounded on a mere caprice will miserably collapse. So we should be moved towards the Name of Jesus under the guidance of the Holy Spirit; then the invocation of the Name will be in us a fruit of the Spirit itself.

17. There is no infallible sign that we are called to the way of the name. There may be, however, some indications of this call, which we ought to consider humbly and carefully. If we feel drawn towards the invocation of the Name, if this practice produces in us an increase of charity, purity, obedience and peace, if the use of other prayers even is becoming somewhat difficult, we may, not unreasonably, assume that the way of the Name is open to us.

18. Anyone who feels the attraction of the way of the Name ought to be careful not to depreciate other forms of prayer. Let us not say: 'The invocation of the Name is the best prayer'. The best prayer is for everybody the prayer to which he or she is moved by the Holy Spirit, whatever prayer it may be. He who practises the invocation of the Name must also curb the temptation of an indiscreet and premature propaganda on behalf of this form of prayer. Let us not hasten to say to God: 'I will declare thy name unto thy brethren',[8] if he is not especially entrusting us with this mission. We should rather humbly keep the secrets of the Lord.

19. What we may say with soberness and truth is this. The invocation of the Name of Jesus simplifies and unifies our spiritual life. No prayer is simpler than this 'one-word prayer' in which the Holy Name becomes the only focus of the whole life. Complicated methods often tire and dissipate thought. But the Name of Jesus easily gathers everything into itself. It has a power of unification and integration. The divided personality which could say: 'My name is legion, for we are many'[9] will recover its wholeness in the sacred Name: 'U*nite* my heart to fear thy name'.[10]

20. The invocation of the Name of Jesus ought not to be understood as a 'mystical way' which might spare us the ascetical purifications. There is no short cut in spiritual life. The way of the Name implies a constant watch over our souls. Sin has to be avoided. Only there are

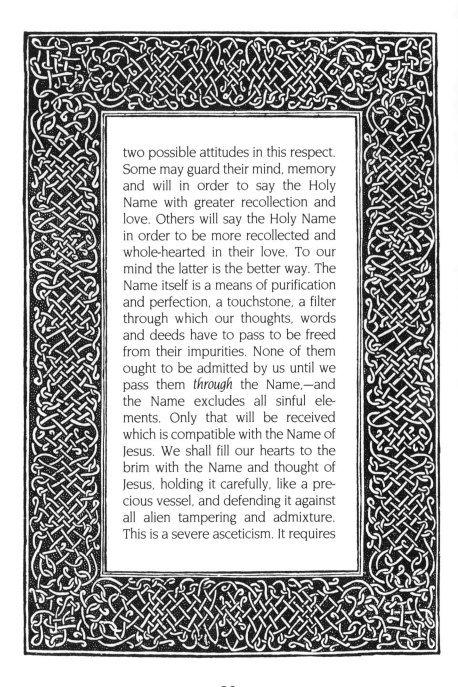

two possible attitudes in this respect. Some may guard their mind, memory and will in order to say the Holy Name with greater recollection and love. Others will say the Holy Name in order to be more recollected and whole-hearted in their love. To our mind the latter is the better way. The Name itself is a means of purification and perfection, a touchstone, a filter through which our thoughts, words and deeds have to pass to be freed from their impurities. None of them ought to be admitted by us until we pass them *through* the Name,—and the Name excludes all sinful elements. Only that will be received which is compatible with the Name of Jesus. We shall fill our hearts to the brim with the Name and thought of Jesus, holding it carefully, like a precious vessel, and defending it against all alien tampering and admixture. This is a severe asceticism. It requires

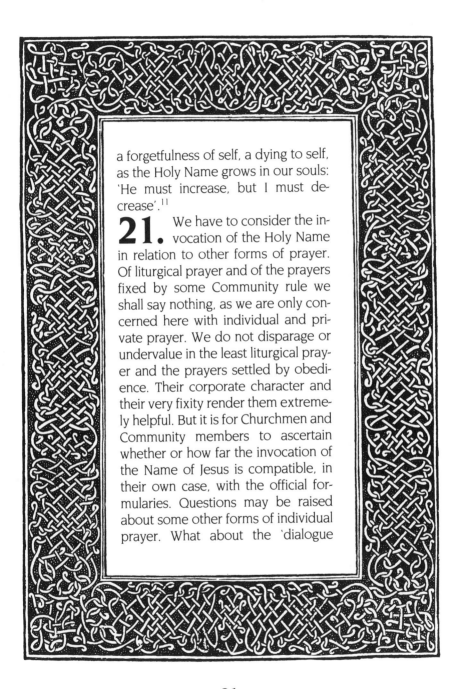

a forgetfulness of self, a dying to self, as the Holy Name grows in our souls: 'He must increase, but I must decrease'.[11]

21. We have to consider the invocation of the Holy Name in relation to other forms of prayer. Of liturgical prayer and of the prayers fixed by some Community rule we shall say nothing, as we are only concerned here with individual and private prayer. We do not disparage or undervalue in the least liturgical prayer and the prayers settled by obedience. Their corporate character and their very fixity render them extremely helpful. But it is for Churchmen and Community members to ascertain whether or how far the invocation of the Name of Jesus is compatible, in their own case, with the official formularies. Questions may be raised about some other forms of individual prayer. What about the 'dialogue prayer', in which we listen and speak to God? What about the purely contemplative and wordless prayer, 'prayer of quiet' and 'prayer of union'? Must we leave these for the invocation of the Holy Name, or inversely? Or should we use both? The answer must be left for God to give in each individual case. In some rare cases the divine call to the invocation of the Name may be exclusive of all other forms of prayer. But we think that, generally speaking, the way of the Name is broad and free; it is, in most cases, perfectly compatible with moments of listening to the inner Word and answering it and with intervals of complete inner silence. Besides we must never forget that the best form of prayer which we can make at any given moment is that to which we are moved by the Holy Spirit.

22. The advice and discreet guidance of some spiritual 'elder' who has a personal experience of the way of the Name may very often be found useful by the beginner. We personally would recommend resort to some such conductor. It is, however, not indispensible. 'When the Spirit of truth is come, he will guide you into all truth'.[12]

IV.
The Invocation of the Name as Worship

I will glorify thy name for evermore.
Psalm 86:12.

23. We have considered until now the invocation of the Name of Jesus in a general manner. Now we must consider the diverse aspects of this invocation. The first aspect is adoration and worship.

24. Too often our prayers are limited to petition, intercession and repentance. As we shall see the Name of Jesus can be used in all these ways. But the disinterested prayer, the praise given to God because of His own excellency, the regard directed towards Him with the utmost respect and affection, the exclamation of Thomas: 'My Lord and my God!'—this ought to come first.

25. The invocation of the Name of Jesus must bring Jesus to our mind. The Name is the symbol and bearer of the Person of Christ. Otherwise the invocation of the Name would be mere verbal idolatry. 'The letter killeth, but the spirit giveth life.'[13] The presence of Jesus is the real content and the substance of the Holy Name. The Name both signifies Jesus' presence and brings its reality.

26. This leads to pure adoration. As we pronounce the Name, we should respond to the presence of Our Lord. 'They ... fell down and worshipped him.'[14] To pronounce thoughtfully the Name of Jesus is to know the allness of Our Lord and our own nothingness. In this knowledge we shall adore and worship. 'God also hath highly exalted him and given him a name which is above every name: that at the name of Jesus every knee should bow'.[15]

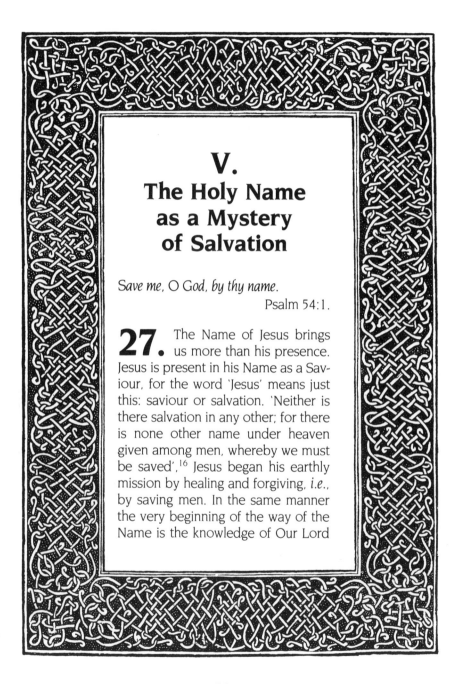

V.
The Holy Name as a Mystery of Salvation

Save me, O God, by thy name.

Psalm 54:1.

27. The Name of Jesus brings us more than his presence. Jesus is present in his Name as a Saviour, for the word 'Jesus' means just this: saviour or salvation. 'Neither is there salvation in any other; for there is none other name under heaven given among men, whereby we must be saved',[16] Jesus began his earthly mission by healing and forgiving, *i.e.*, by saving men. In the same manner the very beginning of the way of the Name is the knowledge of Our Lord as our personal Saviour. The invocation of the Name brings deliverance to us in all our necessities.

28. The Name of Jesus not only helps us to obtain the fulfilment of our needs ('Whatsoever ye shall ask the Father in my name, he will give it to you. Hitherto have ye asked nothing in my name: ask, and ye shall receive').[17] But the Name of Jesus already supplies our needs. When we require the succour of Our Lord we should pronounce his Name in faith and hope, believing that we already receive in it what we ask for. Jesus Himself is the supreme satisfaction of all men's needs. And He is that now, as we pray. Let us not regard our prayer in relation to fulfilment in the future, but in relation to fulfilment *in Jesus now*. He is more than the giver of what we and others need. He is also the gift. He is both giver and gift, containing in Himself all good things. If I hunger he is my food. If I am cold he is my warmth. If I am ill he is my health. If I am persecuted he is my deliverance. If I am impure he becomes my purity. He 'is made unto us ... righteousness, and sanctification and redemption'.[18] This is quite another thing than if he had merely given them to us. Now we may find in his Name all that he is. Therefore the Name of Jesus, in so far as it links us with Jesus Himself, is already a mystery of salvation.

29. The Name of Jesus brings victory and peace when we are tempted. A heart already filled with the Name and presence of Our Lord would not let in any sinful image or thought. But we are weak, and often our defenses break down, and then temptation rises within us like angry waters. In such case do not consider the temptation, do not argue with your own desire, do not

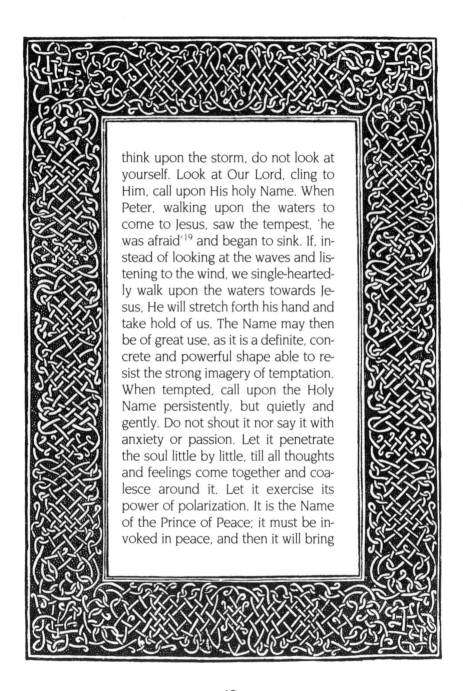

think upon the storm, do not look at yourself. Look at Our Lord, cling to Him, call upon His holy Name. When Peter, walking upon the waters to come to Jesus, saw the tempest, 'he was afraid'[19] and began to sink. If, instead of looking at the waves and listening to the wind, we single-heartedly walk upon the waters towards Jesus, He will stretch forth his hand and take hold of us. The Name may then be of great use, as it is a definite, concrete and powerful shape able to resist the strong imagery of temptation. When tempted, call upon the Holy Name persistently, but quietly and gently. Do not shout it nor say it with anxiety or passion. Let it penetrate the soul little by little, till all thoughts and feelings come together and coalesce around it. Let it exercise its power of polarization. It is the Name of the Prince of Peace; it must be invoked in peace, and then it will bring us peace, or better still, it will (like Him whose symbol it is) be our peace.

30. The Name of Jesus brings forgiveness and reconciliation. When we have grievously sinned (and so much the more when we have sinned lightly), we can, within one second, cling to the Holy Name with repentance and charity and pronounce it with our whole heart, and the Name thus used (and through which we have reached the person of Christ) will already be a token of pardon. After sin let us not 'hang about', delay and linger. Let us not hesitate to take up again the invocation of the Name, in spite of our unworthiness. A new day is breaking and Jesus stands on the shore. 'When Simon Peter heard that it was the Lord he ... cast himself into the sea'.[20] Act like Simon. Say 'Jesus', as though beginning life afresh. We sinners shall find our Lord anew at the invocation of His Name. He comes to us at that moment and as we are. He begins again where He has left us or, rather, where we have left Him. When He appeared to the disciples after the Resurrection, He came to them as they were—unhappy, and lost, and guilty—and without reproaching them with their past defection, He simply entered anew into their every-day life. ' ... He said unto them: 'Have ye here any meat?' And they gave him a piece of broiled fish and of an honeycomb'.[21] In the same manner, when we say 'Jesus' again, after an act of sin or a period of estrangement, He does not require from us long apologies for the past, but He wants us to mix, as before, His Person and His Name with the detail and routine of our life—with our broiled fish and our honeycomb—and to re-plunge them in the very middle of our existence.

31. Thus the Holy Name can bring about reconciliation after our actual sins. But it can give us a more general and fundamental experience of the divine forgiveness. We can pronounce the Name of Jesus and put into it the whole reality of of the cross, the whole mystery of the atonement. If we link the Name with faith in Jesus as propitiation for the sins of all men, we find in the Holy Name the sign of the Redemption extended to all times and to the whole universe. Under this Name we find 'the lamb slain from the foundation of the world',[22] 'the lamb of God which taketh away the sin of the world'.[23]

32. All this does not gainsay or tend to lessen the objective means of penitence and remission of sins offered to us by the Church. We are here only concerned with the hid-

den life of the soul. What we have in view is the inner absolution which repentance produced by charity, already obtains, the absolution which the publican received after his prayer in the temple and of which the Gospel says: 'This man went down to his house justified'.[24]

VI.
The Name of Jesus and the Incarnation

And the Word became flesh.

John 1:14.

33. We have considered the 'saving' power of the Holy Name; we must now go further. In proportion as the Name of Jesus grows within us, we grow in the knowledge of the divine mysteries. The Holy Name is not only a mystery of salvation, the fulfilment of our needs, the abatement of our temptations, the forgiveness of our sins. The invocation of the Name is also a means of applying to ourselves the mystery of the Incarnation. It is a powerful means of union with Our

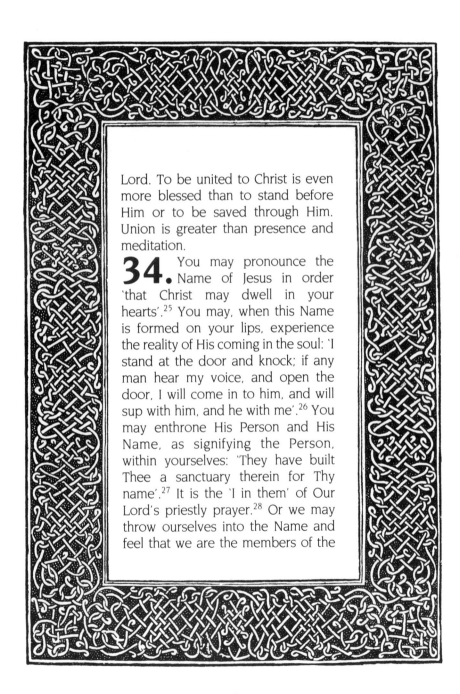

Lord. To be united to Christ is even more blessed than to stand before Him or to be saved through Him. Union is greater than presence and meditation.

34. You may pronounce the Name of Jesus in order 'that Christ may dwell in your hearts'.[25] You may, when this Name is formed on your lips, experience the reality of His coming in the soul: 'I stand at the door and knock; if any man hear my voice, and open the door, I will come in to him, and will sup with him, and he with me'.[26] You may enthrone His Person and His Name, as signifying the Person, within yourselves: 'They have built Thee a sanctuary therein for Thy name'.[27] It is the 'I in them' of Our Lord's priestly prayer.[28] Or we may throw ourselves into the Name and feel that we are the members of the

48

Body of Christ and the branches of the true vine. 'Abide in me'.[29] Of course nothing can abolish the difference between the Creator and the creature. But there is, made possible by the Incarnation, a real union of mankind and of our own persons with Our Lord,—a union which the use of the Name of Jesus may express and strengthen.

35. Some analogy exists between the Incarnation of the Word and the indwelling of the Holy Name within us. The Word was made flesh. Jesus became man. The inner reality of the Name of Jesus, having passed into our souls, overflows into our bodies. 'Put ye on the Lord Jesus Christ'.[30] The living content of the Name enters physically into ourselves. 'Thy Name is as ointment poured forth'.[31] The Name, if I repeat it with faith and love, becomes a strength able to paralyse and over-

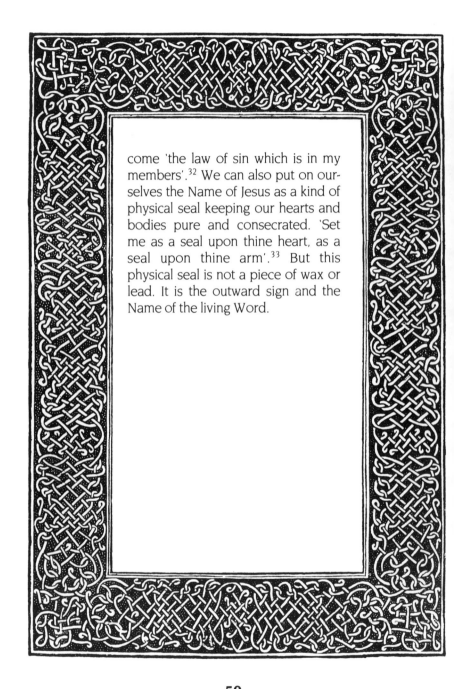

come 'the law of sin which is in my members'.[32] We can also put on ourselves the Name of Jesus as a kind of physical seal keeping our hearts and bodies pure and consecrated. 'Set me as a seal upon thine heart, as a seal upon thine arm'.[33] But this physical seal is not a piece of wax or lead. It is the outward sign and the Name of the living Word.

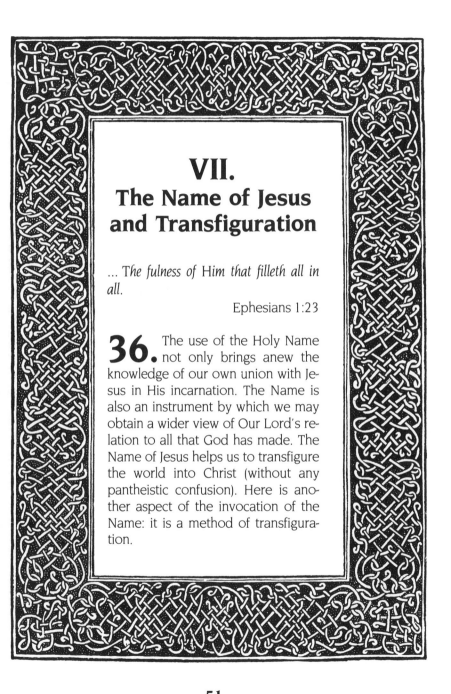

VII.
The Name of Jesus and Transfiguration

... The fulness of Him that filleth all in all.

Ephesians 1:23

36. The use of the Holy Name not only brings anew the knowledge of our own union with Jesus in His incarnation. The Name is also an instrument by which we may obtain a wider view of Our Lord's relation to all that God has made. The Name of Jesus helps us to transfigure the world into Christ (without any pantheistic confusion). Here is another aspect of the invocation of the Name: it is a method of transfiguration.

37. It is so in regard to nature. The natural universe may be considered as the handiwork of the Creator: ' ... the Lord that made heaven and earth'.[34] It can be considered as the visible symbol of the invisible divine beauty: 'The heavens declare the glory of God'.[35] 'Consider the lilies of the field ...'[36] And yet all this is insufficient. Creation is not static. It moves, striving and groaning, towards Christ as its fulfilment and end. 'The whole creation groaneth and travaileth in pain'[37] till it be 'delivered from the bondage of corruption into the glorious liberty of the children of God'.[38] What we call the inanimate world is carried along by a Christward movement. All things were converging towards the Incarnation. The natural elements and the products of the earth, rock and wood, water and oil, corn and wine, were to acquire a new meaning and

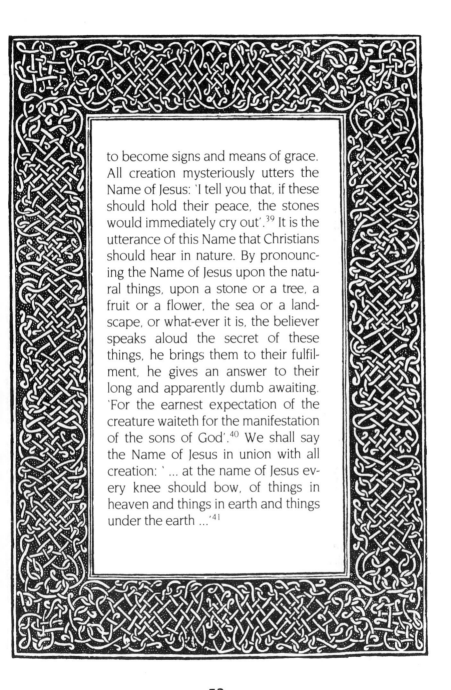

to become signs and means of grace. All creation mysteriously utters the Name of Jesus: 'I tell you that, if these should hold their peace, the stones would immediately cry out'.[39] It is the utterance of this Name that Christians should hear in nature. By pronouncing the Name of Jesus upon the natural things, upon a stone or a tree, a fruit or a flower, the sea or a landscape, or what-ever it is, the believer speaks aloud the secret of these things, he brings them to their fulfilment, he gives an answer to their long and apparently dumb awaiting. 'For the earnest expectation of the creature waiteth for the manifestation of the sons of God'.[40] We shall say the Name of Jesus in union with all creation: ' ... at the name of Jesus every knee should bow, of things in heaven and things in earth and things under the earth ...'[41]

38. The animal world may also be transfigured by us. When Jesus remained forty days in the wilderness, he 'was with the wild beasts'.[42] We do not know what happened then, but we may be assured that no living creature is left untouched by Jesus' influence. Jesus himself said of the sparrows that 'not one of them is forgotten before God'.[43] We are like Adam when he had to give a name to all the animals. 'Out of the ground the Lord God formed every beast of the field, and every fowl of the air, and brought them unto Adam to see what he would call them'.[44] Scientists call them as they think fit. As to us, if we invoke the Name of Jesus upon the animals, we give them back their primitive dignity which we so easily forget—the dignity of living beings being created and cared for by God in Jesus and for Jesus, 'That was the

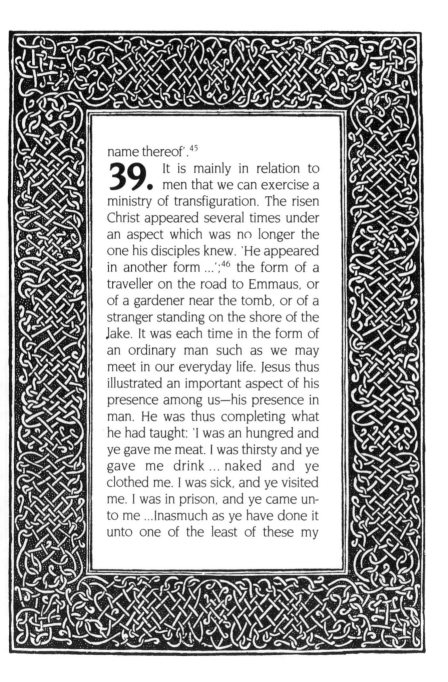

name thereof'.[45]

39. It is mainly in relation to men that we can exercise a ministry of transfiguration. The risen Christ appeared several times under an aspect which was no longer the one his disciples knew. 'He appeared in another form ...';[46] the form of a traveller on the road to Emmaus, or of a gardener near the tomb, or of a stranger standing on the shore of the lake. It was each time in the form of an ordinary man such as we may meet in our everyday life. Jesus thus illustrated an important aspect of his presence among us—his presence in man. He was thus completing what he had taught: 'I was an hungred and ye gave me meat. I was thirsty and ye gave me drink ... naked and ye clothed me. I was sick, and ye visited me. I was in prison, and ye came unto me ...Inasmuch as ye have done it unto one of the least of these my

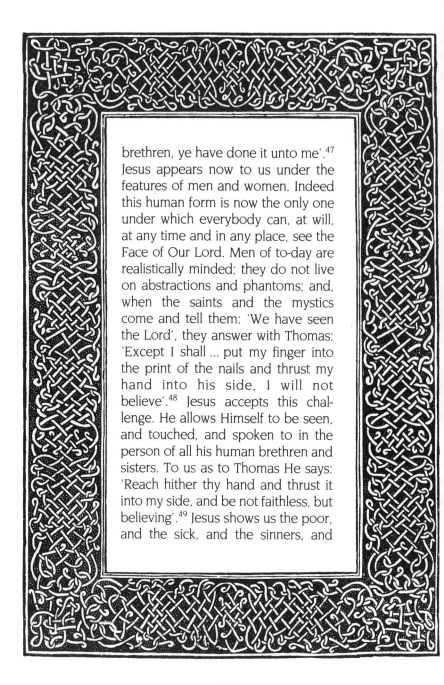

brethren, ye have done it unto me'.[47]
Jesus appears now to us under the
features of men and women. Indeed
this human form is now the only one
under which everybody can, at will,
at any time and in any place, see the
Face of Our Lord. Men of to-day are
realistically minded; they do not live
on abstractions and phantoms; and,
when the saints and the mystics
come and tell them: 'We have seen
the Lord', they answer with Thomas:
'Except I shall ... put my finger into
the print of the nails and thrust my
hand into his side, I will not
believe'.[48] Jesus accepts this chal-
lenge. He allows Himself to be seen,
and touched, and spoken to in the
person of all his human brethren and
sisters. To us as to Thomas He says:
'Reach hither thy hand and thrust it
into my side, and be not faithless, but
believing'.[49] Jesus shows us the poor,
and the sick, and the sinners, and

generally all men, and tells us: 'Behold my hands and my feet ... Handle me and see; for a spirit hath not flesh and bones, as ye see me have'.[50] Men and women are the flesh and bones, the hands and feet, the pierced side of Christ—His mystical Body. In them we can experience the reality of the Resurrection and the real presence (though without confusion of essence) of the Lord Jesus. If we do not see Him, it is because of our unbelief and hardheartedness: 'Their eyes were holden that they should not know Him'.[51] Now the Name of Jesus is a concrete and powerful means of transfiguring men into their hidden, innermost, utmost reality. We should approach all men and women—in the street, the shop, the office, the factory, the 'bus, the queue, and especially those who seem irritating and antipathetic—with the Name of Jesus in our heart and on our lips. We should pronounce His Name over them all, for their real name is the Name of Jesus. Name them with his Name, within His Name, in a spirit of adoration, dedication and service. Adore Christ in them, serve Christ in them. In many of these men and women—in the malicious, in the criminal—Jesus is imprisoned. Deliver Him by silently recognizing and worshipping Him in them. If we go through the world with this new vision, saying 'Jesus' over every man, seeing Jesus in every man, everybody will be transformed and transfigured before our eyes. The more we are ready to give of ourselves to men, the more will the new vision be clear and vivid. The vision cannot be severed from the gift. Rightly did Jacob say to Esau, when they were reconciled: 'I pray thee, if now I have found grace in thy sight, then receive my present at my hand,

for therefore I have seen thy face as though I had seen the face of God'.[52]

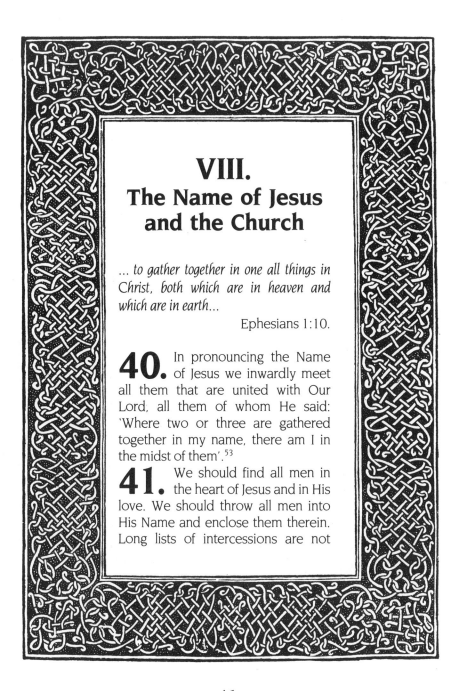

VIII.
The Name of Jesus and the Church

... to gather together in one all things in Christ, both which are in heaven and which are in earth...

Ephesians 1:10.

40. In pronouncing the Name of Jesus we inwardly meet all them that are united with Our Lord, all them of whom He said: 'Where two or three are gathered together in my name, there am I in the midst of them'.[53]

41. We should find all men in the heart of Jesus and in His love. We should throw all men into His Name and enclose them therein. Long lists of intercessions are not

61

necessary. We may *apply* the Name of Jesus to the name of such or such person who is in particular need. But all men and all just causes are already gathered together within the Name of Our Lord. Adhering to Jesus is to become one with Him in His solicitude and loving kindness for them. Adhering to Our Lord's own intercession for them is better than to plead with Him on their behalf.

42. Where Jesus is, there is the Church. Whoever is in Jesus is in the Church. If the invocation of the Holy Name is a means of union with Our Lord, it is also a means of union with that Church which is in Him and which no human sin can touch. This does not mean that we are closing our eyes to the problems of the Church on earth, to the imperfections and disunity of Christians. But we only deal here with this eternal, and spiritual, and 'unspotted'

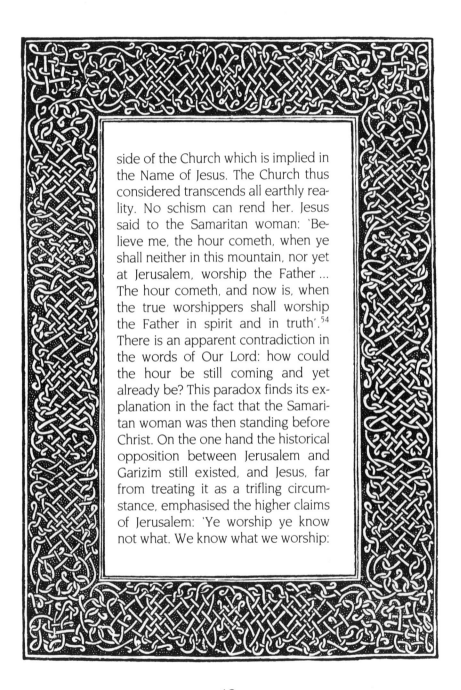

side of the Church which is implied in the Name of Jesus. The Church thus considered transcends all earthly reality. No schism can rend her. Jesus said to the Samaritan woman: 'Believe me, the hour cometh, when ye shall neither in this mountain, nor yet at Jerusalem, worship the Father ... The hour cometh, and now is, when the true worshippers shall worship the Father in spirit and in truth'.[54] There is an apparent contradiction in the words of Our Lord: how could the hour be still coming and yet already be? This paradox finds its explanation in the fact that the Samaritan woman was then standing before Christ. On the one hand the historical opposition between Jerusalem and Garizim still existed, and Jesus, far from treating it as a trifling circumstance, emphasised the higher claims of Jerusalem: 'Ye worship ye know not what. We know what we worship:

for salvation is of the Jews.'[55] In that sense the hour was not yet, but was still coming. On the other hand the hour already was, because the woman had before her Him who is greater than Jerusalem or Garizim, Him who 'will tell us all things'[56] and in Whom alone we can fully 'worship in spirit and in truth'.[57] The same situation arises when, invoking the Name of Jesus, we cling to His Person. Assuredly we do not believe that all the conflicting interpretations of the Gospel which we hear on earth are equally true nor that the divided Christian groups have the same measure of light. But, fully pronouncing the Name of Jesus, entirely surrendered to His Person and His claims, we implicitly share in the wholeness of the Church, and so we experience her essential unity, deeper than all our human separations.

43. The invocation of the Name of Jesus helps us to meet again, in Him, all our departed. Martha was wrong when, speaking of Lazarus, she said to Our Lord: 'I know that he shall rise again in the resurrection at the last day'.[58] Overlooking the present she was projecting all her faith into the future. Jesus corrected her mistake: 'I *am* the resurrection and the life'.[59] The life and the resurrection of the departed is not merely a future event (although the resurrection of the individual bodies is such). The person of the risen Christ already is the resurrection and the life of all men. Instead of trying to establish—in our prayer, or in our memory, or in our imagination—a direct spiritual contact with our departed, we should try to reach them within Christ, where their true life now is. One can, therefore, say that the invocation of the Name of Jesus is the best prayer for the departed. The invocation of the Name, giving us the presence of Our Lord, makes them also present to us. And our linking of the Holy Name with their own names is our work of love on their behalf.

44. These departed, whose life is now hidden with Christ, form the heavenly Church. They belong to the total and eternal Church, of which the Church now militant on earth is but a very small part. We meet in the Name of Jesus the whole company of the Saints: 'His Name shall be in their foreheads'.[60] In it we meet the angels; it is Gabriel who, first on earth, announced the Holy Name, saying to Mary: 'Thou shalt call his name Jesus'.[61] In it we meet the woman 'blessed among women' to whom Gabriel spoke these words and who so often called her son by His name. May the Holy Spirit make us desire to hear the Name of Jesus

as the Virgin Mary first heard it and to repeat that Name as Mary and Gabriel uttered it! May our own invocation of the Name enter this abyss of adoration, obedience and tenderness!

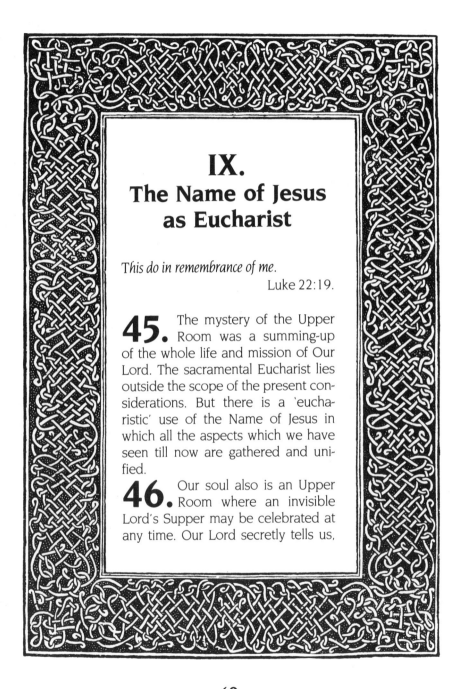

IX.
The Name of Jesus as Eucharist

This do in remembrance of me.

Luke 22:19.

45. The mystery of the Upper Room was a summing-up of the whole life and mission of Our Lord. The sacramental Eucharist lies outside the scope of the present considerations. But there is a 'eucharistic' use of the Name of Jesus in which all the aspects which we have seen till now are gathered and unified.

46. Our soul also is an Upper Room where an invisible Lord's Supper may be celebrated at any time. Our Lord secretly tells us,

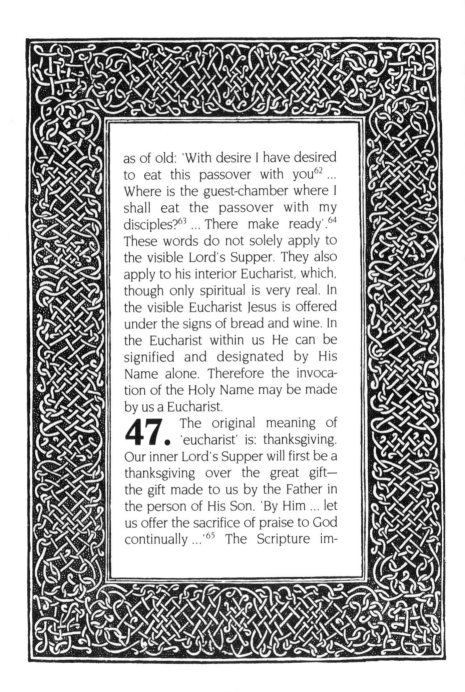

as of old: 'With desire I have desired to eat this passover with you[62] ... Where is the guest-chamber where I shall eat the passover with my disciples?[63] ... There make ready'.[64] These words do not solely apply to the visible Lord's Supper. They also apply to his interior Eucharist, which, though only spiritual is very real. In the visible Eucharist Jesus is offered under the signs of bread and wine. In the Eucharist within us He can be signified and designated by His Name alone. Therefore the invocation of the Holy Name may be made by us a Eucharist.

47. The original meaning of 'eucharist' is: thanksgiving. Our inner Lord's Supper will first be a thanksgiving over the great gift—the gift made to us by the Father in the person of His Son. 'By Him ... let us offer the sacrifice of praise to God continually ...'[65] The Scripture immediately explains the nature of this sacrifice of praise: '... that is, the fruit of our lips giving thanks to His name'. So the idea of the Name is linked with that of thanksgiving. Not only may we, while pronouncing Jesus' Name, thank the Father for having given us His Son or direct our praise towards the Name of the Son Himself, but we may make of the Name of the Son the substance and support of the sacrifice of praise rendered to the Father, the expression of our gratitude and our offering of thanks.

48. Every Eucharist is an offering. 'That they may offer unto the Lord an offering in righteousness'.[66] We cannot offer to the Father a better offering than the person of His Son Jesus. This offering alone is worthy of the Father. Our offering of Jesus to His Father is one with the offering which Jesus is eternally making of Himself, for how could we, alone, offer Christ? In order to give a concrete shape to our offering we shall probably find it helpful to pronounce the Name of Jesus. We shall present the Holy Name to God as though it were bread and wine.

49. The Lord, in His Supper, offered to His disciples bread which was broken and wine which was shed. He offered a life which was given, His body and blood ready for the immolation. When we inwardly offer Jesus to His Father, we shall always offer Him as a victim—both slain and triumphant: 'Worthy is the Lamb that was slain to receive ... honour, and glory, and blessing'.[67] Let us pronounce the Name of Jesus with the awareness that we are washed and made 'white in the blood of the Lamb'.[68] This is the sacrificial use of the Holy Name. This does not mean that we think of a new sacrifice of the cross. The Holy Name, sacrificially used, is but a means to apply to us, here and now, the fruits of the oblation once for all made and perfect. It helps us, in the exercise of the universal priesthood, to make spiritually actual and present the eternal sacrifice of Christ. The sacrificial use of the Name of Jesus will also remind us that we cannot be one with Jesus, priest and victim if we do not offer within Him, within His Name, our own soul and body: 'In burnt offerings and sacrifices for sin thou hast had no pleasure: Then said I, Lo, I come'.[69]

50. There is no Lord's Supper without a communion. Our inner Eucharist also is what tradition has called 'spiritual communion', that is, a feeding by faith on the Body and Blood of Christ without using the visible elements of bread and wine. 'The bread of God is he which cometh down from heaven, and giveth life

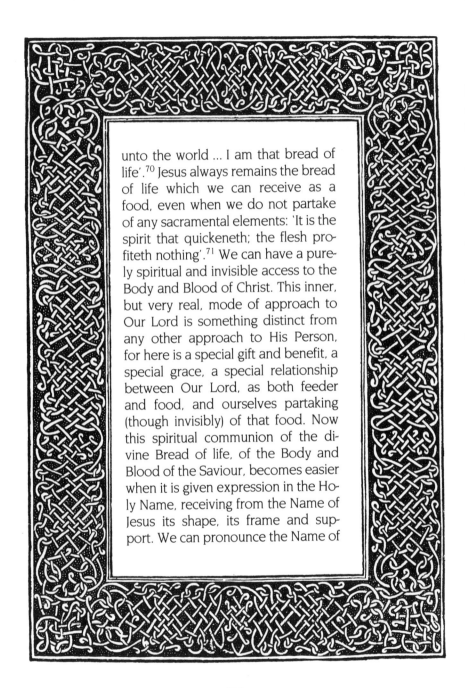

unto the world ... I am that bread of life'.[70] Jesus always remains the bread of life which we can receive as a food, even when we do not partake of any sacramental elements: 'It is the spirit that quickeneth; the flesh profiteth nothing'.[71] We can have a purely spiritual and invisible access to the Body and Blood of Christ. This inner, but very real, mode of approach to Our Lord is something distinct from any other approach to His Person, for here is a special gift and benefit, a special grace, a special relationship between Our Lord, as both feeder and food, and ourselves partaking (though invisibly) of that food. Now this spiritual communion of the divine Bread of life, of the Body and Blood of the Saviour, becomes easier when it is given expression in the Holy Name, receiving from the Name of Jesus its shape, its frame and support. We can pronounce the Name of

Our Lord with the special intention of feeding our soul on it, or rather on the sacred Body and precious Blood which we try to approach through it. Such a communion may be renewed as often as we desire. Far from us the error of treating lightly or lowering in esteem the Lord's Supper as practised in the Church. But it is to be hoped that everybody who follows the way of the Name may experience that the Name of Jesus is a spiritual food and communicates to hungry souls the Bread of life. 'Lord, evermore give us this bread'.[72] In this bread, in this Name, we find ourselves united with all them that share in the same Messianic meal: 'We being many are one bread and one body: for we are all partakers of that one bread'.[73]

51. Through the Eucharist we 'do shew the Lord's death till he come'.[74] The Eucharist is an an-

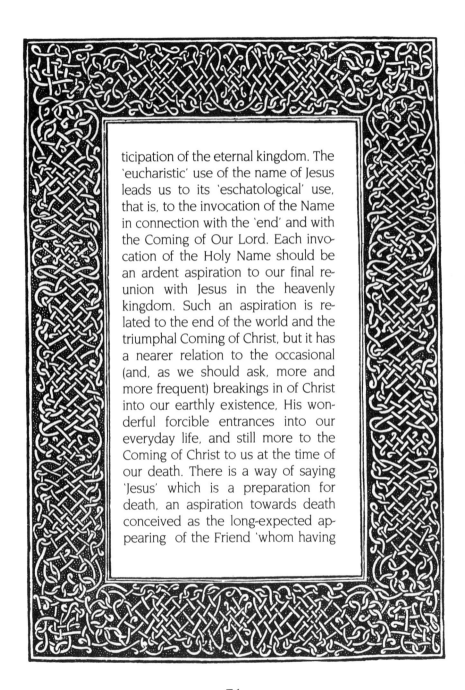

ticipation of the eternal kingdom. The 'eucharistic' use of the name of Jesus leads us to its 'eschatological' use, that is, to the invocation of the Name in connection with the 'end' and with the Coming of Our Lord. Each invocation of the Holy Name should be an ardent aspiration to our final reunion with Jesus in the heavenly kingdom. Such an aspiration is related to the end of the world and the triumphal Coming of Christ, but it has a nearer relation to the occasional (and, as we should ask, more and more frequent) breakings in of Christ into our earthly existence, His wonderful forcible entrances into our everyday life, and still more to the Coming of Christ to us at the time of our death. There is a way of saying 'Jesus' which is a preparation for death, an aspiration towards death conceived as the long-expected appearing of the Friend 'whom having not seen, ye love'.[75] a call for this supreme meeting and here and now a throwing of our heart beyond the barrier. In that way of saying 'Jesus', the longing utterance of Paul, 'When Christ, who is our life, shall appear ...'[76] and the cry of John, 'Come, Lord Jesus',[77] are already implied.

X.
The Name of Jesus and the Holy Spirit

I saw the Spirit descending from heaven like a dove, and it abode upon him.

John 1:32

52. The Name of Jesus occupied a pre-eminent place in the message and action of the Apostles. They were preaching in the Name of Jesus, healing the sick in His Name; they were saying to God: 'Grant unto thy servants ... that signs and wonders may be done by the name of thy holy child Jesus'.[78] Through them 'the name of the Lord Jesus was magnified'.[79] It is only after Pentecost that the Apostles announced the Name 'with power'. Je-

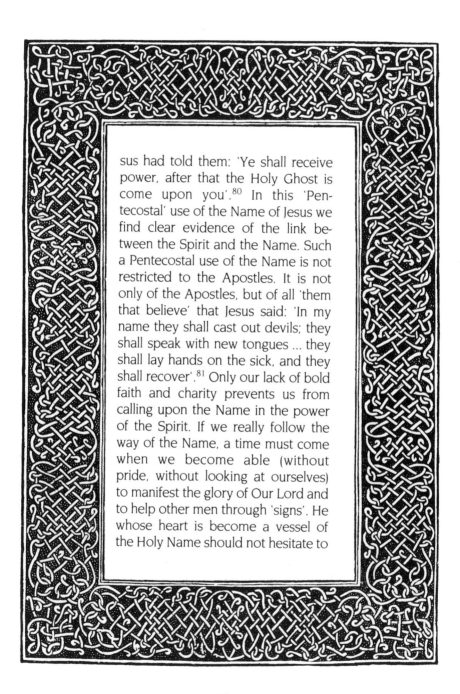

sus had told them: 'Ye shall receive power, after that the Holy Ghost is come upon you'.[80] In this 'Pentecostal' use of the Name of Jesus we find clear evidence of the link between the Spirit and the Name. Such a Pentecostal use of the Name is not restricted to the Apostles. It is not only of the Apostles, but of all 'them that believe' that Jesus said: 'In my name they shall cast out devils; they shall speak with new tongues ... they shall lay hands on the sick, and they shall recover'.[81] Only our lack of bold faith and charity prevents us from calling upon the Name in the power of the Spirit. If we really follow the way of the Name, a time must come when we become able (without pride, without looking at ourselves) to manifest the glory of Our Lord and to help other men through 'signs'. He whose heart is become a vessel of the Holy Name should not hesitate to go about and repeat to those who need spiritual or bodily relief the words of Peter: 'Silver and gold have I none; but such as I have give I thee: in the name of Jesus Christ of Nazareth rise up and walk'.[82] O that the Spirit of Pentecost may come and write within us the Name of Jesus in flame!

53. The Pentecostal use of the Name is but one aspect of our approach to the Holy Ghost through the Name of Jesus. The name will lead us to some other and more inward experiences of the Spirit. While pronouncing the Name we may obtain a glimpse of the relationship between the Spirit and Jesus. There is a certain attitude of the Spirit towards Jesus and a certain attitude of Jesus towards the Spirit. In repeating the Name of Jesus we find ourselves at the cross-roads, so to speak, where these two 'movements' meet.

54. When Jesus was baptized 'the Holy Ghost descended in bodily shape like a dove upon Him'.[83] The descent of the dove is the best expression of the attitude of the Spirit towards Our Lord. Now let us, while saying the Name of Jesus, try to coincide, if we may say so, with the Jesus-ward movement of the Spirit, with the Spirit directed by the Father towards Jesus, looking to Jesus, coming to Jesus. Let us try to unite ourselves—as much as a creature can unite itself to a divine action—to this flight of the dove ('Oh that I had wings like a dove ...'[84]) and to the tender feelings expressed by her voice: 'The voice of the turtle is heard in our land'.[85] Before making 'intercession for us with groanings which cannot be uttered',[86] the Spirit was and eternally remains sighing after Jesus. The book of Revelation shows us the Spirit, together with the bride (that is,

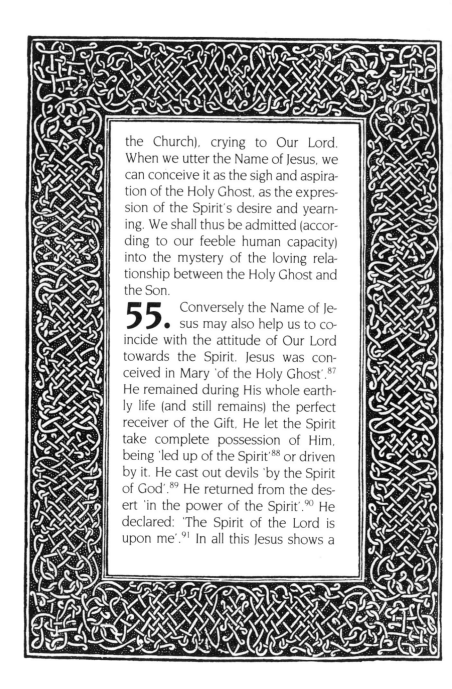

the Church), crying to Our Lord. When we utter the Name of Jesus, we can conceive it as the sigh and aspiration of the Holy Ghost, as the expression of the Spirit's desire and yearning. We shall thus be admitted (according to our feeble human capacity) into the mystery of the loving relationship between the Holy Ghost and the Son.

55. Conversely the Name of Jesus may also help us to coincide with the attitude of Our Lord towards the Spirit. Jesus was conceived in Mary 'of the Holy Ghost'.[87] He remained during His whole earthly life (and still remains) the perfect receiver of the Gift, He let the Spirit take complete possession of Him, being 'led up of the Spirit'[88] or driven by it. He cast out devils 'by the Spirit of God'.[89] He returned from the desert 'in the power of the Spirit'.[90] He declared: 'The Spirit of the Lord is upon me'.[91] In all this Jesus shows a humble docility towards the Holy Ghost. In pronouncing the Name of Jesus we can (as far as is given to man) make ourselves one with Him in this surrender to the Spirit. But we can also make ourselves one with Him as with the starting point from which the Spirit is sent to men: 'He shall take of mine, and shall shew it unto you[92] ... I will send him unto you'.[93] We can see the Name of Jesus as the focus from which the Spirit radiates towards mankind; we can see Jesus as the mouth from which the Spirit is breathed. Thus, in the utterance of the Name of Jesus, we can associate ourselves with these two moments: the filling of Jesus with the Spirit, the sending of the Spirit by Jesus. To grow in the invocation of the Holy Name is to grow in the knowledge of the 'Spirit of his Son'.[94]

XI.
The Name of Jesus and the Father

He that hath seen me hath seen the Father.

John 14:9

56. Our reading of the Gospel will remain superficial as long as we only see in it a message directed to men or a life turned towards men. The very heart of the Gospel is the hidden relationship of Jesus with the Father. The secret of the Gospel is Jesus turned towards Him. This is the fundamental mystery of the life of Our Lord. The invocation of the Name of Jesus may afford us some real, though faint and transient, partaking in that mystery.

57. 'In the beginning was the Word'.[95] The Person of Jesus is the living Word spoken eternally by the Father. As the Name of Jesus, by a special divine dispensation, has been chosen to mean the living Word uttered by the Father, we may say that this Name partakes to some extent in this eternal utterance. In a somewhat anthropomorphic manner (easy to correct) we might say that the Name of Jesus is the only human word which the Father eternally pronounces. The Father eternally begets His Word. He gives Himself eternally in the begetting of the Word. If we endeavour to approach the Father through the invocation of the Name of Jesus, we have first, while pronouncing the Name, to contemplate Jesus as the object of the Father's love and self-giving. We have to feel (in our little way) the outpouring of this love and this gift on the Son. We have already seen the dove descending upon Him. It remains to hear the Father's voice saying: 'Thou art my beloved son; in thee I am well pleased'.[96]

58. And now we must humbly enter into the filial consciousness of Jesus. After having in the word 'Jesus' the Father's utterance: 'My son!', we ought to find in it the Son's utterance: 'My Father!' Jesus has no other aim than to declare the Father and be His Word. Not only have all Jesus' actions, during His earthly life, been acts of perfect obedience to the Father ('My meat is to do the will of him that sent me'[97]); not only has the sacrificial death of Jesus fulfilled the supreme requirement of the divine love (of which the Father is the source): 'Greater love hath no man than this, that a man lay down his life ...'[98]—not only the deeds of Jesus, but His whole being were the perfect expression of the Father. Jesus is 'the brightness of his glory, and image of his person'.[99] The Word was 'towards God'[100]—the translation 'with God' is inaccurate. It is this eternal orientation of the Son towards the Father, his eternal turning to Him, which we should experience within the Name of Jesus. There is more in the Holy Name than the 'turning to' the Father. In saying 'Jesus' we can in some measure join together the Father and the Son, we can realize and appropriate their oneness. At the very moment when we utter the Holy Name, Jesus Himself says to us as He said to Philip: 'Believest thou not that I am in the Father and the Father in me? ... Believe me that I am in the Father, and the Father in me'.[101]

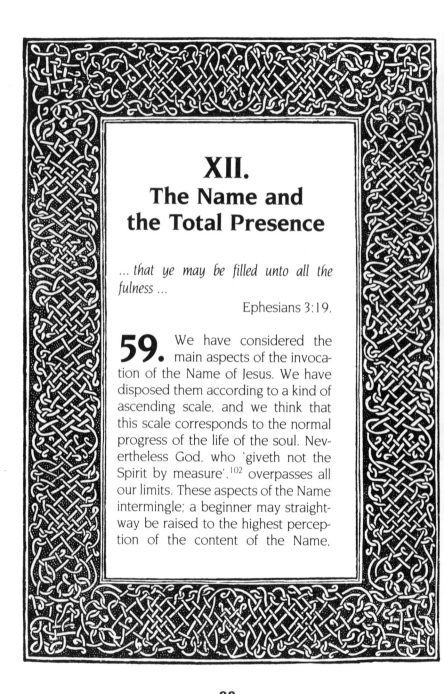

XII.
The Name and the Total Presence

... that ye may be filled unto all the fulness ...

Ephesians 3:19.

59. We have considered the main aspects of the invocation of the Name of Jesus. We have disposed them according to a kind of ascending scale, and we think that this scale corresponds to the normal progress of the life of the soul. Nevertheless God, who 'giveth not the Spirit by measure'.[102] overpasses all our limits. These aspects of the Name intermingle; a beginner may straightway be raised to the highest perception of the content of the Name,

while somebody who has been waiting on the Name for years may not
go beyond the elementary stages (it
is not this that matters, the only thing
that matters is to do what Our Lord
wants us to do). So the pattern which
we have followed is, to a large extent, artificial and has but a relative
value.

60. This becomes quite evident
to anybody who has had
some experience of all the aspects of
the Name which have been de-
scribed here. At that stage—the
reaching of which does not necessari-
ly imply a greater perfection, but
often some intellectual and spiritual
acumen, some quickness of perception and discrimination concerning
the things of God—it becomes difficult, even wearisome and tedious,
and sometimes even impossible, to
concentrate on this or that particular
aspect of the Name of Jesus, how-

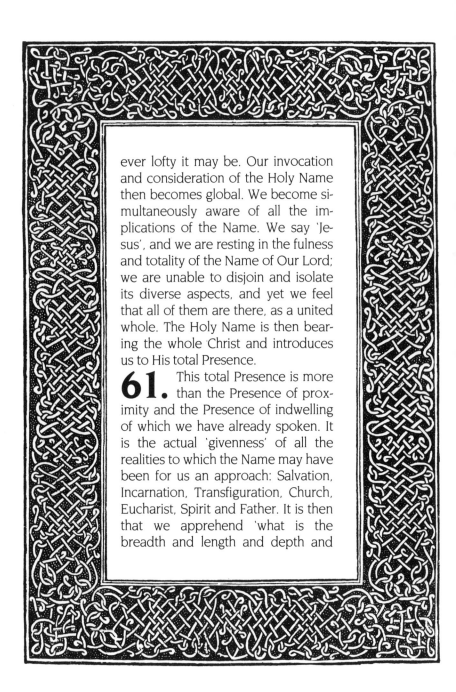

ever lofty it may be. Our invocation and consideration of the Holy Name then becomes global. We become simultaneously aware of all the implications of the Name. We say 'Jesus', and we are resting in the fulness and totality of the Name of Our Lord; we are unable to disjoin and isolate its diverse aspects, and yet we feel that all of them are there, as a united whole. The Holy Name is then bearing the whole Christ and introduces us to His total Presence.

61. This total Presence is more than the Presence of proximity and the Presence of indwelling of which we have already spoken. It is the actual 'givenness' of all the realities to which the Name may have been for us an approach: Salvation, Incarnation, Transfiguration, Church, Eucharist, Spirit and Father. It is then that we apprehend 'what is the breadth and length and depth and

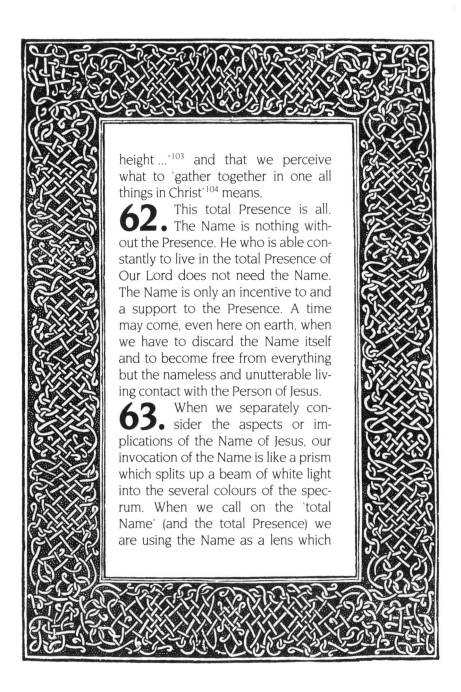

height ...'[103] and that we perceive what to 'gather together in one all things in Christ'[104] means.

62. This total Presence is all. The Name is nothing without the Presence. He who is able constantly to live in the total Presence of Our Lord does not need the Name. The Name is only an incentive to and a support to the Presence. A time may come, even here on earth, when we have to discard the Name itself and to become free from everything but the nameless and unutterable living contact with the Person of Jesus.

63. When we separately consider the aspects or implications of the Name of Jesus, our invocation of the Name is like a prism which splits up a beam of white light into the several colours of the specrum. When we call on the 'total Name' (and the total Presence) we are using the Name as a lens which

91

receives and concentrates the white light. Through the means of a lens a ray of the sun can ignite some combustible substance. The Holy Name is this lens. Jesus is the burning Light which the Name, acting as a lens, can gather and direct till a fire is kindled within us. 'I am come to send fire on the earth ...'[105]

64. The Scripture often promises a special blessing to them that call on the Name of the Lord. We may apply to the Name of Jesus what is said of the Name of God. We shall therefore repeat: 'Look thou upon me, and be merciful unto me, as thou usest to do unto those that love thy name'.[106] And of every one of us may the Lord say what he said of Saul: 'He is a chosen vessel unto me, to bear my name ...'[107]

AMEN.

FOOTNOTES

1. Matthew 6:6.
2. I. Corinthians 12:3.
3. I. Kings 19:13.
4. Song of Songs 5:2.
5. Matthew 9:21.
6. Genesis 32:26.
7. Song of Songs 1:3-4.
8. Psalm 22:22.
9. Mark 5:9.
10. Psalm 86:11.
11. John 3:30.
12. John 16:13.
13. II. Corinthians 3:6.
14. Matthew 2:11.
15. Philippians 2:9-10.
16. Acts 4:12.
17. John 16:23-24.
18. I. Corinthians 1:30.
19. Matthew 14:30.
20. John 21:7.
21. Luke 24:41-42.
22. Revelation 13:8.
23. John 1:29.
24. Luke 18:24.
25. Ephesians 3:17.
26. Revelation 3:20.

27. II. Chronicles 20:8.
28. John 17:26.
29. John 15:4.
30. Romans 13:14.
31. Song of Songs 1:3.
32. Romans 7:23.
33. Song of Songs 8:6.
34. Psalm 134:3.
35. Psalm 19:1.
36. Matthew 6:28.
37. Romans 8:22.
38. Romans 8:21.
39. Luke 19:40.
40. Romans 8:19.
41. Philippians 2:10.
42. Mark 1:13.
43. Luke 12:6.
44. Genesis 2:19.
45. Genesis 2:19.
46. Mark 16:12.
47. Matthew 25:35-36, 40.
48. John 20:25.
49. John 20:27.
50. Luke 24:39.
51. Luke 24:16.
52. Genesis 33:10.
53. Matthew 18:20.
54. John 4:21, 23.

55. John 4:22.
56. John 4:25.
57. John 4:24.
58. John 11:24.
59. John 11:25.
60. Revelation 22:4.
61. Luke 1:31.
62. Luke 22:15.
63. Luke 22:11.
64. Luke 22:12.
65. Hebrews 13:15.
66. Malachi 3:3.
67. Revelation 5:12.
68. Revelation 7:14.
69. Hebrews 10:6-7.
70. John 6:33, 48.
71. John 6:63.
72. John 6:34.
73. I. Corinthians 10:17.
74. I. Corinthians 11:26.
75. I. Peter 1:8.
76. Colossians 3:4.
77. Revelation 22:20.
78. Acts 4:29, 30.
79. Acts 19:17.
80. Acts 1:8.
81. Mark 16:17-18.
82. Acts 3:6.

83. Luke 3:22.
84. Psalm 55:6.
85. Song of Songs 2:12.
86. Romans 8:26.
87. Matthew 1:20.
88. Matthew 4:1.
89. Matthew 12:28.
90. Luke 4:14.
91. Luke 4:18.
92. John 16:15.
93. John 16:7.
94. Galatians 4:6.
95. John 1:1.
96. Luke 3:22.
97. John 4:34.
98. John 15:13.
99. Hebrews 1:3.
100. John 1:1.
101. John 14:10, 11.
102. John 3:34.
103. Ephesians 3:18.
104. Ephesians 1:10.
105. Luke 12:49.
106. Psalm 119:132.
107. Acts 9:15.